Maltese T

Joseph Vella.

ISBN: 9781982914479

Delicious Maltese Cooking.

The Purpose of this Book is to Encourage Healthy eating.

Delicious Cooking The Maltese Way As Taught by Maltese Mothers and Granma's of Old.

Enjoy!

Maltese Traditional Recipes

Baked Lampuki (Baked Fish) - Page 6

Baked Macaroni - Page 7

Baked stuffed Marrows - Page 8-9

Baked Rice - Page 10

Beef Stew - Page 11

Bigilla (spicy broad Beans) - Page 12

Bigilla - Page 13

Brodu (Mums Maltese Soup) - Page 14

Bragioli I-Forn (Baked Beef Olives) - Page 15

Bragioli (Stuffed Steak) - Page 16

Bragioli (Beef Rolls) - Page 17

Choux Pastry with Ricotta - Page 18

Fenek Mogli (Fried Rabbit) - Page 19

Maltese Traditional Recipes

Figolli (Maltese Easter biscuits) - Page 20

Green Pepperoni Stuffed with Tuna - Page 21

Hobz (Maltese Bread) - Page 22

Lampuki Fritters (Fried Fish) - Page 23

Lampuki Pie (Fish Pie) - Page 24

Lampuki with Green Pepper Sauce (Fish) - Page 25

Macaronelli with Ricotta - Page 26

Maltese Pastizzi - Page 27

Maltese Ravioli (Ricotta Pastry) - Page 28

Marrows Stuffed with Mince Meat - Page 29

Meat Pie - Page 30

Minestra (Thick Vegetable Soup) - Page 31

Octopus Stew - Page 32

Maltese Traditional Recipes

Porpetti (Maltese Patties) - Page 33

Puddina (Bread Pudding) - Page 34

Ricotta Pie - Page 35

Risotto with Sea Food - Page 36

Ruggata (Orzata - Almond Soft Drink Cordial) - Page 37

Smoked salmon and prawn macaroni cheese - Page 38

Spaghetti Biz-zalza tal-qarnit (In octopus sauce) - Page 39

Spinach and Ricotta Pie - Page 40

Stuffed Skirt Steak (falda tac-canga mimlija) - Page 41

Split Pea and Ham Soup - Page 42-43

Stuffat Tal-fenek (Rabbit Stew) - Page 44

Stuffat Tal-qarnit (Octopus Stew) - Page 45

Stuffed Egg-plant - Page 46

Maltese Traditional Recipes

Stuffed Globe Artichokes - Page 47

Thick Vegetable Soup - Page 48

Timpana (Baked Macaroni in a Pastry Case) - Page 49

Tomato Sauce with Meat and Eggs - Page 50

Vegetable Soup with Meat - Page 51

Village Biscuits - Page 52

White Bait Poupiettes (Fish Patties) - Page 53

Widow's Soup - Page 54

Maltese Traditional Recipes

B aked Lampuki (Baked Fish)

Ingredients.

4 medium sized Lampuki

40g peeled onions

3/4 kg peeled potatoes

Little water

Fennel seeds

Marjoram

Garlic

Oil

Method.

1 Clean and wash the fish. Cut the potatoes and onions into thick slices. Peel the garlic.

2 Prepare a baking dish with a layer of potatoes and onions.

3 Put the fish one near the other on this bed of potatoes and onions.

4 Crush garlic on the fish, season and sprinkle some marjoram. Cover with the remainder of potatoes and onions, season and sprinkle some fennel seeds.

Maltese Traditional Recipes

B aked Macaroni

Ingredients

400g macaroni

2 hard boiled eggs

600ml beef stock

100g onions

50g tomato paste

50g grated cheese

200g minced meat
3 eggs

Seasoning
Oil, 1 Peel and chop the onions and fry them in a little oil until they obtain a golden colour.

Method

1 Add meat and continue cooking until it is brown.
2 Add tomato paste and stock and cook for a further 20 minutes.
3 Boil macaroni in plenty of salted water. When this is ready, drain off the water.
4 Add meat sauce, cheese, chopped hard boiled eggs, eggs and seasoning to the macaroni. Blend everything.

5 Prepare a greased pie dish. Put the macaroni in this dish and cook for 40-40 minutes in a medium to hot oven.

Maltese Traditional Recipes

Baked stuffed Marrows

I baked it with onions & potatoes

So it is a complete meal.

Ingredients

6 large round marrows, stem cut, washed and take the inside pulp out, using a teaspoon. You can use it with the filling if you wish.

750 g minced lamb or minced meat of your choice.

1 large finely chopped onion.

4 tablespoons tomato paste.

1/2 cup tomato passata. (You use tomato puree instead of Passata)

3 finely chopped garlic cloves.

2 tablespoons grated cheese.

1/2 cup finely chopped parsley.

1 beaten egg.

Seasoning. 2 bay leaves. 1/2 teaspoon mixed spice. 1/2 teaspoon ground cinnamon.

For the onions & potatoes you need: 2 large onions cut into slices. About 8 good sized potatoes peeled and sliced. 4 garlic cloves. Fennel seeds. Seasoning.

Method: In a saucepan fry the finely chopped onion and when it's soft add the cinnamon and mixed spice. Then add the minced meat & garlic and fry until brown. **Continue next page.**

Maltese Traditional Recipes

Mix in the tomato paste and cook it for a few minutes. Add the passata, season well with black pepper and salt and 2 bay leaves.

And let it simmer for about 20 minutes. Turn off and uncover so it cools a bit. While the stuffing is simmering, peel the potatoes and onions.

In another saucepan or large deep frying pan, heat some oil and fry the sliced onions. Add the sliced potatoes & garlic mix with the onion and fry for a few minutes.

Season well with salt and pepper, add 2 cups water, cover and simmer. I prefer to cook it a bit so it will not take too long in the oven.

Put over low heat and cook until the potatoes are sort of half cooked. Take care what potatoes you use because some type of potatoes cook faster than others.

Remove the bay leaves from the minced meat stuffing,

Add the grated cheese, chopped parsley and beaten egg.

Mix well. Then fill the marrows with this mixture.

When potatoes are ready, spread in a baking dish. Sprinkle some fennel or caraway seeds on top.

Over it place the stuffed marrows.

You can sprinkle some more grated cheese or fine breadcrumbs or even semolina on top of the stuffed marrows.

Bake in preheated 200C oven until the marrows are done and the potatoes are a bit crunchy.

Maltese Traditional Recipes

Baked Rice

Ingredients

250g rice

25g grated cheese

50g tomato paste

100g peeled tomatoes

250g minced meat

300ml stock

4 eggs, Olive oil

Salt and pepper

Method

1 Cook the meat. Add the chopped tomatoes and tomato paste. Add the stock and simmer for 30 minutes.

2 Wash rice and boil in salted water. When half cooked strain and cool under running water.

3 Mix the rice well with the sauce and the other ingredients.

4 Put the mixture into a greased baking dish and cook in a moderate oven for 45 minutes.

Maltese Traditional Recipes

Beef Stew

Ingredients

600g beef (rump or topside)

125g peeled tomatoes

150g peas

150g onions

40g tomato paste

1lt water or stock

Pinch of mixed spice

Flour

Oil, Salt and pepper

Method

1 Slice the meat. Pass the meat through the flour and fry. When golden brown remove from pan and put into a casserole.

2 Fry the chopped onions.

3 Chop the tomatoes and add all the ingredients to the meat. Bring to the boil and simmer for 1½ hours

Maltese Traditional Recipes

B igilla (spicy broad *Beans*)

Ingredients

1 lb dried broad beans

2 sprigs parsley

1 head of garlic crushed

1 chilli pepper

A dash of Tabasco

1 tbsp of mixed marjoram & mint,

Finely chopped

2 tbsp olive oil

Method

Soak beans overnight
Replace water.
Add salt to taste
Bring to boil & simmer until beans are soft
Mash beans lightly and place them in a serving dish
Pour olive oil on top
Add other ingredients to taste

Maltese Traditional Recipes

Bigilla

Ingredients

400g dried beans

Vinegar

Chilli pepper

Bicarbonate of soda

Plenty of garlic cloves

Chopped parsley

Olive oil

Method

1 Soak the beans in salted water with some bicarbonate of soda for 24 hours.

2 Wash beans and cook them in plenty of salted water.
Bring to the boil and simmer till they are cooked. Do not leave the beans short of water, as they may stick to the bottom of the pan and burn.

3 Mince beans. Season and add some olive oil and put into a serving dish.

4 Chop the parsley, crush the garlic and chilli pepper; mix with some oil and vinegar.

Pour this sauce over the beans.

Maltese Traditional Recipes

B rodu (Mums Maltese Soup)

It's all very easy to make. Just don't overdo the water content. And the most important ingredient is the celery.
I have tweaked the recipe a bit to make it easier. Still tastes just as good. If you don't use the skirt steak it might taste a little bit different, but close enough. The soup will last in the fridge easy for 4-5 days.

Ingredients
2 whole Skirt steaks cut into quarters.
(If you can't get them use chuck steak or any stewing steak, or you can do 1 skirt and 2 pieces of chicken legs or thighs).
The chicken does give it more flavour.
1 onion finely chopped, - 1 carrot finely chopped.

1-2 large potatoes peeled but left whole (this is so you can put in the porpetti if you want to make them, otherwise chop them in quarters)
1 large stick celery chopped.
2 sticks celery left whole (just for flavour)
l liters liquid either chicken, beef or vegetable stock (I prefer beef)
1 heaped tablespoon tomato paste
About 3-3 1/2 liters of cold tap water. Salt and pepper.
One cup basmati rice (put in for the last 12 minutes of cooking only)

Method:
Put all the ingredients in the pot except for the rice, bring to the boil, and then simmer on low for at least one hour and up to 1 ½ hours. Simmer with lid on the pot, if the lid has a flat top with a rim around put in about ½ cup water on the lid and keep topping up as it evaporates, this stops the liquid inside the pot from reducing put in the rice for the last 12 minutes to cook.
Stir occasionally throughout the cooking time.
You can either eat the meat separately or make porpetti.
To continue to make Porpetti. Look at the recipe in this book.

Maltese Traditional Recipes

B ragioli I-Forn (Baked Beef Olives)

Ingredients
8 very thin slices of beef (for 4 persons)
3 hard boiled eggs
8 slices of streaky bacon
4 sausages (preferably Maltese)
Cheddar Cheese (optional)
One red onion
Fresh garlic
Fresh parsley
1 pint of Ale.
Salt and Pepper

Method
1 Chop the eggs, bacon, sausages and cheddar cheese and mix in a bowl.
2 Add salt, pepper and fresh parsley, if no Maltese sausage was found, you may add some Coriander Seeds

Method
3 Open a slice of beef and place approx. 2 tablespoons of mixture towards the edge of the steak
4 Roll the steak and fold (like a Spring Roll)
5 Stick a tooth-pick right through, to hold the fold
6 Preheated oven (half)
7 In a large frying pan heat some oil, and fry the beef olives with some garlic, till blood is slightly drained
8 Prepare a medium sized dish, and place the beef olives side by side in this dish
9 Slice the onion and place in dish
10 Drown half the beef olives in beer and add salt and pepper to taste.
11 Cover with baking foil and put in preheated oven for about 45 mins.
12 Uncover the dish and cook for a further 30 mins. You may serve with traditional baked potatoes

Maltese Traditional Recipes

B ragioli (Stuffed Steak)

Ingredients
Mince with herbs and flavourings are rolled inside and then cooked gently in a tomato based sauce. This can also be served as two meals, using the sauce with pasta as a first course.
6 thin slices of topside or round steak, flattened with a mallet
400g veal mince
2 rashers bacon, diced
2 cloves garlic, crushed
½ cup parsley, finely chopped
1 tbsp oregano, finely chopped
1 shallot, thinly sliced
½ cup gbejniet (Maltese cheese), grated
2 eggs, beaten

Method Sauce
3 tbsp olive oil, 2 large onions, diced, 5 cloves garlic, crushed.

Method
1 tin tomato
1 cup flat leaf parsley leaves picked
½ cup basil leaves picked. - 250ml red wine.
500ml water-Salt and pepper to taste-2 bay leaves
1. To make sauce, fry onion and garlic in olive oil until softened.
2. Add tomatoes, herbs, red wine and water and leave to simmer while you prepare the bragioli.
3. Lay out beef slices.
4. Mix remaining ingredients together and season with salt and pepper.
5. Place a heaped tablespoon of stuffing mixture on each beef slice, spreading out well.
6. Roll up and secure with skewers, toothpicks or tie with Butcher's twine.
7. Place in sauce and simmer for 1 ½ hours over low heat.

Maltese Traditional Recipes

B ragioli (Beef Rolls)

Ingredients
10 thin slices of rump steak
Stuffing
1/2 lb ground beef
6 bacon strips
2 hard-boiled eggs
2 tbsp chopped parsley
4 tbsp bread crumbs
1 carrot grated
Pepper and salt
Sauce:
2 large onions, chopped
3 garlic cloves, crushed
4 tomatoes, peeled and chopped
1 tsp tomato paste
2 carrots, scraped and sliced
1/2 cup peas 2 potatoes, peeled and quartered 2 bay leaves 1 tsp Worcestershire sauce 1/2 cup red wine

Method
In a bowl combine all stuffing ingredients.
Pound and flatten slices of steak.
Spoon about 2 tbsp of stuffing on each meat slice. Roll up slice.
Use string or toothpicks to secure rolled-up meat.
In a saucepan cook for a few minutes onion and garlic in enough water to cover onion.
Add beef rolls and brown over medium heat.
Remove beef rolls from saucepan and set aside.
Add potatoes, tomatoes, carrots, tomato paste, herbs, and wine to Sauce pan. Add pepper and salt to taste. Stir gently and cook for about 10 minutes. Return beef rolls in saucepan, add peas and bring to boil.
Reduce heat and simmer to thicken sauce. Add wine if mixture begins to dry up before meat is thoroughly cooked.

Maltese Traditional Recipes

Choux Pastry with Ricotta

Ingredients

This is a traditional sweet dish.

200g ricotta

50g chopped candied cherries

100g sugar

Honey

Chopped nuts

Oil for frying

For Choux Pastry

Flour, Margarine, Pinch of sugar
Water, Eggs.

Method

1 Make the choux pastry and pipe small profiteroles.

2 Deep fry in hot oil till golden.

When ready leave to cool.

3 Slit and fill with ricotta, sugar and chopped candied cherries.

4 Dip the top of the pastry in honey and sprinkle with chopped nuts

Maltese Traditional Recipes

F<u>enek</u> <u>Mogli</u> (Fried Rabbit)

Ingredients

1 Rabbit
Sunflower Oil
Fresh Garlic
Dry White Wine
Thyme
Pepper

Method

1. Cut rabbit in medium sized pieces
2. Chop some garlic
3. In a large bowl place the rabbit and cover with white wine
4. Mix in the garlic, Thyme, and add some salt and pepper

Method

5. Cover and leave in the fridge overnight or for approx. 6 hrs

6. In a large shallow frying pan heat some sunflower oil.

7. Add some garlic to the oil and fry for a few minutes on moderate heat (do not fry till golden brown)

8. Take the rabbit pieces and fry in large frying pan, turning occasionally, till rabbit cooks well.

9. You may add salt, pepper and thyme (or your favourite herb)

10. Sprinkle more white wine occasionally.

11. Rabbit may be served with French fries and salad.

Maltese Traditional Recipes

Figolla

Ingredients

For the Pastry
480g flour, 120g sugar, 300g margarine
2 eggs, grated orange zest

For the Filling

200g ground almonds, 150g sugar, 2 egg whites,
Water to cover, Icing sugar, Small Easter eggs.

Method
1 Rub the flour and margarine to a sandy texture. Mix the eggs, sugar and orange zest. Add to the flour and form dough. Leave to set for 1 hour before using it.
2 Put the sugar in a deep pan, just cover with water and bring to the boil. Add the ground almonds and mix well. Leave to set.

Method
3 Roll out the pastry and cut into different shapes (using fancy shape cutters). Cut two pieces of each shape.

4 Put the first piece of the pastry on a baking sheet; spread some of the almond mixture in the centre. Wet the edges, and put the other piece of the pastry on top of it. Press the edges to seal.

5 Bake in a moderate oven for 25 to 30 minutes.
6 Prepare the royal icing.
7 Decorate the figolla when cold.
Put the Easter egg in the centre.

This is an Easter speciality especially favoured by the children. Figolli are made in different shapes, but the most important item in the figolla is the chocolate egg.

Maltese Traditional Recipes

Green Pepperoni Stuffed with Tuna

Ingredients

4 large green peppers

100g chopped onions

150g rice

1 tin of tuna

25g tomato paste

Mint

Olive oil, some water
Salt and pepper

Method

1 Cut the top of each pepper and removes the seeds.

2 Wash and boil the rice.

3 Fry onions till golden brown, add tuna, mint and tomato paste. Season...

4 Add water and simmer for 5 to 8 minutes.

5 Drain rice and mix well with the sauce. Stuff the peppers with the rice   mixture.

6 Put peppers in well greased pie dish and bake for 35 to 45 minutes.

Maltese Traditional Recipes

H**obz** (Maltese Bread)

Ingredients

600g flour

10g salt

15g sugar

15g margarine

25g yeast

345ml Luke warm water

1 tablespoon milk

Method

1 Mix the flour, salt and margarine. Add the yeast.
2 Make a mixture of the Luke warm water, sugar and the milk.
3 Add on to the flour and knead the mixture well until the dough is white and   elasticized.
4 Place in a bowl, seal with cling film and a wet dish towel, place in a warm place for about 1 hour.
5 Work the dough, cut into small pieces (50g). Place on a baking tray, paste with egg, cut with a knife and let the pieces rest for about 15 minutes.
6 Cook in oven 450F (232C) gas mark 6-8 for 12-15 minutes.

Maltese Traditional Recipes

Lampuki Fritters (or any Frying Fish)

Ingredients

Lampuki (Fish)
Olive oil
Garlic
Mint
Oil for frying
Flour

Seasoning For the batter

250ml milk
20g flour
10g yeast Salt

Method

1 Clean the fish and fillet cutting into small pieces.

2 in a small bowl marinate fish in chopped garlic, olive oil, mint and seasoning. Leave for 2 hours.

3 Prepare the batter by mixing the flour, salt and yeast. All lukewarm milk, stir and leave to set in a warm place for 1 hour.

4 Remove the fish from the marinate, pass through the flour, batter and fry in plenty of hot oil till golden brown.

5 Serve hot with tomato sauce.

Maltese Traditional Recipes

Lampuki Pie (Fish Pie)

Ingredients

750g Lampuki

250g peeled and chopped tomatoes
250g boiled cauliflower

250g tomato purée
200g chopped onions

150g peas, 100g black olives
200g cooked spinach, 2 eggs, Olive oil,

Fresh mint, lemon zest, Garlic,
Sesame seeds, salt and pepper,
Short or puff pastry.

Method

1 Clean the fish and steam or boil. Leave to cool and remove all bones.

2 Heat some oil, fry the onions and garlic and cook to a light golden colour.

3 Add the peas, chopped cauliflower, spinach, olives, tomatoes, tomato paste, and zest of lemon, salt, pepper and mint. Cook for a few minutes. And add the eggs.
4 Line a greased pie dish with pastry.
5 Fill in with the Lampuki mixture.
6 Moisten the edges and cover with pastry.
7 Egg wash... Sprinkle some sesame and cook in a moderate to hot oven for 50 minutes.

Maltese Traditional Recipes

Lampuki with Green Pepper Sauce (Fish)

Ingredients

1kg Lampuki

½kg peeled tomatoes

200g chopped onions

½kg green pepper

25g tomato paste

Olive oil, Mint and Garlic
Flour, Lemon zest

Method

1 Clean the fish, remove head and tail. Cut into small pieces, about 8cm long. Pass through seasoned flour and fry on both sides in hot olive oil. Cook till done.

2 Clean and roughly slice the green pepper. Fry in a little oil till crisp.

3 in a separate pan fry the onions and garlic; add the mint, tomatoes and tomato paste. Simmer for 15 minutes. Add the finely chopped zest and seasoning. Add this sauce to the fried green pepper.

4 Put the fish into the sauce and cook in the oven for 20 minutes. Serve hot.

Maltese Traditional Recipes

Macaronelli with Ricotta

Ingredients

600g Macaronelli

5 eggs

400g ricotta

50g butter

Chopped parsley

Salt and pepper

Method

1 Boil Macaronelli in salted water.
When cooked, drain and put into a clean pan.

2 Mix ricotta, eggs, chopped parsley and seasoning.

3 Add butter to Macaronelli and cook for a few minutes on a very low heat.

4 Add ricotta mixture and continue cooking for about 20 minutes, still on a very low heat.

5 Serve hot.

Maltese Traditional Recipes

Maltese Pastizzi (Ricotta Pastry Case)

Ingredients

2 lbs. flaky pastry dough
2 lbs. ricotta cheese
Salt
2 eggs
Method
Note: You can substitute Pillsbury Flaky Pastry Dough for home-made flaky pastry dough
Mix the ricotta cheese with the two eggs until the eggs are thoroughly mixed into the ricotta cheese.
Add a bit of salt to the mixture for taste.

Method

Roll out the dough (do not make the dough too thin.)
Cut the dough into three- to four-inch circles.
Put one tablespoon of the ricotta cheese mix in the middle of each circle.

Fold each circle from the top and the bottom to the centre and squeeze the edges together so that the pocket is sealed (the horizontal ends should be formed into points.)

Put the Pastizzi on a margarine greased baking sheet.
Bake in a moderate oven (350-425 degrees) for about one hour.

You will need to experiment a bit with the oven temperature and the cooking time. The Pastizzi Best eaten when they are warm with a cup of good coffee or tea. Enjoy!

Maltese Traditional Recipes

Maltese Ravioli (Ricotta Pastry)

Ingredients

For the Dough

200g plain flour, a pinch of salt, 150g semolina, 2 beaten eggs
For the filling:

400g ricotta, salt and pepper

2 eggs beaten

4tbsp grated parmesan cheese

1 tbsp chopped parsley

Method

Mix the sieved flour, semolina and salt carefully, add the eggs and knead until dough is like elastic, if too stiff add a drop of cold water.

Rest the dough for 1 hour and prepare the filling.

Put all the other ingredients ricotta, beaten eggs cheese parsley salt and pepper into a mixing bowl mix everything well.

Divide the dough into 4 pieces and roll into long thin strips dampen the edges with water.

Put small balls of ricotta some 2cm from the edge of the pastry and 4cm apart.

Turn one edge of the pastry on the other one and press to seal; using a ravioli cutter cut out the pastry 10 cms away from the filling. Leave to nest for few minutes, boil in salted water till soft.

Serve with Pasta sauce and grated cheese.

Maltese Traditional Recipes

Marrows Stuffed with Mince Meat

Ingredients

4 large marrows
2 eggs
100g onions
25g tomato paste

600g minced meat

1 kg potatoes

50g grated cheese

Clove of garlic
Chopped parsley

Olive oil, Salt and pepper

Method

1 Cut the marrows' top and scoop the insides. Chop the onions and garlic.

2 Fry in hot oil, taking care not to brown. Add tomato paste and meat. Continue cooking until the meat is cooked. Add the chopped marrow pulp, and cook for a few more minutes. Allow to cool.

3 Add the eggs, cheese, parsley and seasoning. Fill the marrows and place them on a bed of sliced potatoes.

4 Bake for 1 to 1½ hours

Maltese Traditional Recipes

Meat Pie.

Ingredients

1kg pastry either short or puff

125g peeled tomatoes

3 eggs, 200g onions, 125g peas

50g tomato paste

600g minced meat (beef and pork)

50g grated cheese

Water or stock

Salt and pepper, Pinch of mixed spice, Oil

Method

1 Fry the chopped onions; do not brown. Add the meat and continue cooking. Cover with some water or stock.

2 Add the chopped tomatoes, peas, tomato paste, mixed spice, salt and pepper.

Cook for 15 minutes.

3 Remove from the heat, add the eggs and cheese and mix well.

4 Line a well greased pie dish (the dish must not be very deep). Fill it with the mixture, cover with the rest of the pastry, egg wash the top and bake in a moderate oven.

Maltese Traditional Recipes

Minestra (Thick Vegetable Soup)

Ingredients

84g cauliflower

84g carrots

84g pumpkin

56g white onions

28g celery stick

21g tomato paste

56g rice

1250ml water

Method

1 Slice and wash all the vegetables.
2 Fry the onions, till tender.
3 Add all vegetables except the rice.
4 Add the water, bring to the boil, and simmer till vegetables are cooked.
5 Add the washed rice. Soup must be very thick.

Maltese Traditional Recipes

Octopus Stew

Ingredients

800g octopus
100g black olives, sliced
50g tomato paste
600ml red wine
200g potatoes cut into squares
100g onions
150g tomatoes, peeled and chopped
100g peas

Water, Lemon zest and Garlic.

Method

1 Clean octopus and cut into small pieces.
(It is recommended that the fish be beaten with a kitchen hammer before cutting it).

2 Put the octopus into a frying pan, add some
   Water and cook for about 20 minutes.

3 Fry the onions and garlic, add the tomato paste, tomatoes, grated lemon and olives. Simmer.

4 Add the water and bring to the boil.
Add the fish after draining off the water.
Simmer for 1½ hours, and then add the peas, potatoes and wine.

5 Continue cooking till everything is cooked. Great care should be taken when seasoning the stew.

Maltese Traditional Recipes

P<u>orpetti</u> (Maltese Patties)

Ingredients
Take out the cooked skirt steaks and potatoes
From the **previously made Brodu** (soup).

Mince together and place in a bowl,
Add 1 egg,
Some fresh parsley,
Salt and pepper
One clove of finely chopped garlic.

Method

Make into patties,
Lightly dust with flour
Then cook them in a fry pan for about 3-5 minutes on each side in olive oil until golden.

That's it yummy!

A Quick stew (from porpetti).

Ingredients
The other thing you can do with the <u>skirt steak or porpetti</u> is once its cooked, make up a quick stew,

1 chopped onion,
2-3 sliced carrots,
4 quartered potatoes,

Method
Cook in some water to cover, Add some salt, pepper.
 Worcestershire sauce,
1 stock cube,
1 tablespoon tomato paste on low until nearly soft then add 2 tablespoon of gravox mixed in some water,
Add some peas, mushrooms and the skirt steak for about 5 minutes to heat through. Yummy again.

Maltese Traditional Recipes

P**uddina** (Bread Pudding)

Ingredients

Day old bread soaked in water mixed with a generous amount of dried fruit, chocolate and custard powder. Puddina is served in slices with tea or coffee as an afternoon snack.

1 loaf day-old bread
375g sugar
2 tbsp custard powder
2 tbsp corn flour
4 tbsp cocoa
2 eggs, beaten
500g mixed dried fruit
250g almonds
250g glace cherries, halved
Vanilla to taste
4 tbsp whisky, brandy or sherry

Method

Day old bread soaked in water mixed with a generous amount of dried fruit, chocolate and custard powder. Puddina is served in slices with tea or coffee as an afternoon snack.

1 loaf day-old bread
375g sugar
2 tbsp custard powder
2 tbsp corn flour
4 tbsp cocoa
2 eggs, beaten
500g mixed dried fruit
250g almonds
250g glace cherries, halved
Vanilla to taste . 4 tbsp whisky, brandy or sherry.

Maltese Traditional Recipes

Ricotta Pie

Ingredients

600g ricotta

50g grated cheese

3 eggs

Salt and pepper

Puff pastry or short crust pastry

Chopped parsley

Egg wash

Method

1 Mix ricotta with eggs and work to a smooth mixture. Add cheese, parsley and seasoning.

Check seasoning as it is very important to get the flavour right, because it will be almost impossible to correct it after baking the pie.

2 Grease a pie or sandwich tin, line with pastry and fill with ricotta. Eggs wash the edges and cover with pastry.

3 Egg wash and bake in a moderate oven until a nice golden colour is reached. Serve warm.
 (This pie can also be cooked without the pastry cover).

Risotto with Sea Food

Ingredients

400g rice

500g fresh clams

500g fresh mussels

100g chopped onions

1.5ml water

Chopped parsley

Mint

Olive oil, Salt and pepper

Method

1 Heat some oil and fry the onions to a light colour. Add the rice and continue frying for 3 minutes. Add water, bring to boil and simmer for 15 minutes.

2 Cook the mussels and clams, remove shell and add the rice, season preferably using fresh ground pepper (if you want substitute the fresh mussels and clams with tinned ones, use 150g of each).

3 Continue cooking for another 10 minutes or until the rice is nicely cooked.

4 Garnish with chopped parsley before serving.

Maltese Traditional Recipes

Ruggata (Almond Cordial)

Traditional almond refreshing drink with water

There are plenty of ways to make this Almond Cordial. I think this is pretty close to the real thing.

Ingredients

500 grams Barley powder.

100 mills Almond essence.

250 grams white sugar.

2 litres water.

Method

1. Put barley in water and boil for 30 mins.

2. Let cool and drain well. Using just the liquid.

3. Add the essence and sugar and boil again for another 30 mins, making sure that the sugar has melted.

4. Cool and put mixture in glass bottles and place in a refrigerator.

With this cordial, use the same as normal to make a refreshing cool drink.

Maltese Traditional Recipes

Smoked salmon and prawn macaroni cheese

Ingredients

500g macaroni
1 Onion

500g smoked Salmon
3 tbs flour

1 fish stock cube
500ml skimmed milk

500g penne
500g thawed Prawns

1 mugful of milk
One white gbejna (goat cheeselet)

Method

In a pan cook one chopped onion and 500g chopped smoked salmon; remove from heat add 3 tbs flour;

Add one fish stock cube, and 500ml skimmed milk;
Put on a low heat and stir till a thick sauce forms.

Boil 500g Macaroni (and stir in the sauce; add 500g frozen thawed prawns;

Pour one mugful of milk onto the macaroni mix;

Grate one white gbejna (Tasty Cheese) and sprinkle on top;
Bake in a moderate oven (160 fan electric/ 170 gas) for about 30 minutes or till golden brown.

Maltese Traditional Recipes

Spaghetti Biz-zalza tal-qarnit (Spaghetti with octopus sauce)

Ingredients

1kg Octopus
224g onions

168g peas
224g tomatoes

112g black olives
250ml red wine

674g spaghetti
84g tomato paste
Herbs
Mint
Lemon zest
Olive oil
Salt and pepper

Method

1 Peel and slice the onions. Cut the octopus into even sized pieces, fry in a little oil and water.
2 Add the tomato paste and herbs continue cooking for about 20 minutes.
3 Prepare the tomato concise, by peeling the tomatoes and chopping them finely, add to the onions.
4 Strain the octopus but save the liquid. Slice the olives and lemon zest.
5 Add all remaining ingredients to the first mixture and simmer for a while.
6 Add the octopus liquid and simmer for another 15 minutes.
7 Cook spaghetti for not more than 7 minutes or till it is al dente

Maltese Traditional Recipes

Spinach and Ricotta Pie

Ingredients
For the Pastry
Flour
Margarine
Pinch of salt
Water

For the Filling

500g ricotta
80g grated cheese
150g ham
800g spinach
2 eggs
Egg white
Salt and pepper

Method

1 Clean and wash the spinach. Boil in salted water. When cooked remove as much water as possible.

2 Cut ham into small pieces. Mix ricotta, egg, ham, chopped spinach, salt, pepper and cheese. Mix well.

3 Grease a pie dish and line with pastry. Fill in with the mixture. Egg wash the edge and covers with pastry. Make some pastry decoration on top.

4 Egg wash and bake in a moderate oven for about 45 minutes.

Maltese Traditional Recipes

Stuffed Skirt Steak (Flank)

Ingredients

1 kilo Skirt (Flank) Steak

350g minced meat

1 tbsp olive oil

3 garlic cloves, finely chopped

6 tbsp breadcrumbs

200g Grated Tasty Cheese (Hanini Gibniet Nixfin)

300g can Mayor Processed Peas

2 eggs, beaten, a mug of boiling water, Salt & Pepper.

Method

In a bowl mix the minced meat with the garlic cloves, the processed peas, breadcrumbs, grated cheese, salt, pepper and eggs and delicately stuff inside the flank steak.

Sew the meat up.

Warm the oil in a large pan and fry the meat until cooked on the outside.

After add the boiling water and simmer for an hour.

Serve with some boiled vegetables and roasted potatoes.

Maltese Traditional Recipes

Split Pea and Ham Soup

Ingredients

2 tablespoons unsalted butter

1 large onion, chopped fine (about 1 1/2 cups)
Table salt

2 medium garlic cloves, minced or pressed through garlic press (about 2 teaspoons)

7 cups water

1 ham steak (about 3/4 pound), skin removed

3 slices thick-cut bacon (about 4 ounces)

1 pound green split peas (about 2 cups), picked through and rinsed

2 sprigs fresh thyme

2 bay leaves

2 medium carrots, peeled and cut into 1/2-inch pieces (about 1 cup)

1 medium celery rib, cut into 1/2-inch pieces (about 1 cup)

Ground black pepper

Method

Heat butter in large Dutch oven over medium-high heat.

When foaming subsides, add onion and ½ teaspoon salt; Cook, stirring frequently, until softened, about 3 to 4 minutes.

Add garlic and cook until fragrant, about 30 seconds.

Continue next Page.

Maltese Traditional Recipes

Add water, ham steak, bacon, peas, thyme, and bay leaves.

Increase heat to high and bring to simmer, stirring frequently to
Keep peas from sticking to bottom.

Reduce heat to low, cover, and simmer until peas are tender but not
falling apart, about 45 minutes.

Remove ham steak, cover with foil or plastic wrap to prevent drying
out, and set aside.

Stir in carrots and celery; continue to simmer, covered, until
vegetables are tender and peas have almost completely broken
down, about 30 minutes longer.

When cool enough to handle,
Shred ham into small bite-size pieces with two forks.

Remove and discard thyme sprigs, bay leaves, and bacon slices.

Stir ham back into soup and return to simmer.

Season to taste with salt and pepper;
Serve the soup sprinkled with Buttery Croutons and chopped mint.

Maltese Traditional Recipes

Stuffat Tal-fenek (Rabbit Stew)

Ingredients

1 rabbit
2 onions, sliced
6 garlic cloves, peeled
3 large tomatoes, peeled and chopped
2 tsp tomato paste
3 potatoes, peeled and quartered
6 carrots peeled and sliced
1 cup peas
2 bay leaves
Mixed herbs
1 tsp olive oil
1 stock cube
Salt and pepper
1 1/4 cups red wine
Flour

Method

1. Add salt and pepper to flour. Mix well.

2. Roll rabbit portions in seasoned flour.

3. Cook rabbit in olive oil until slightly brown.

4. Add onions, garlic, tomatoes and potatoes to the pot.

Pour some of the wine over the ingredients.
Add tomato paste, stock cube and bay leaves.

5. Add kidney, liver and peas. Bring to a boil and simmer for about 1 1/2 hours. Add more wine if sauce begins to dry up.

Maltese Traditional Recipes

Stuffat Tal-qarnit (Octopus Stew)

Ingredients

1 1/2 lb octopus
2 tbsp oil

3 onions, chopped
1/2 lb peas

3 garlic cloves, crushed
2 tbsp tomato paste

1 carrot, grated
8 black olives

Pinches of: basil, oregano, mint
1 cup of red wine

Dash of Worcestershire sauce
Pepper to taste

Method

Cut octopus into bite-size pieces.
Slightly cook onion and garlic in oil in a pot.
Add octopus and the other ingredients.
Cook for about an hour over medium heat or until octopus is tender.

This stew may be served hot over spaghetti or it may be cooked as a main course by adding 1 lb of peeled and quartered potatoes at the beginning of cooking time.

Maltese Traditional Recipes

Stuffed Egg-plant

Ingredients

2 medium sized egg-plants

75g onions

50g tomato paste

25g grated cheese

400g minced meat (pork or beef)

2 eggs

Salt and pepper

Method

1 Cut the egg-plants in half (lengthwise) and boil for 6 minutes. Remove the pulp from their centre and chop it.

2 Fry the onions, add meat and the chopped egg-plant. Cook for 10 minutes, add tomato paste, salt and pepper.

3 Remove from the heat, adding eggs and cheese. Stuff the egg-plants with this mixture.

4 Bake in a hot oven for 35 to 40 minutes.

Maltese Traditional Recipes

Stuffed Globe Artichokes

Ingredients

4 Artichokes
75g anchovy fillets

Crushed Garlic
150g fresh breadcrumbs

50g Olives,
Oil and Vinegar, Parsley

Salt and pepper

Method

Chop the anchovy fillets, garlic, olives and parsley and mix with the breadcrumbs.

Add the oil and vinegar and work into a dry paste. Season.

Wash the artichokes and fill between the leaves with this mixture.

3. Place the artichokes upright in a small saucepan.
Half cover them with water and add some oil.

Cover with a lid, bring to boil and simmer for 1 hour.
Serve hot.

Maltese Traditional Recipes

Thick Vegetable Soup

Ingredients

100g cauliflower
50g white onions

1¼ lit water

100g pumpkin
25g tomato paste

100g carrots
25g celery stick

25g grated cheese

50g fine pasta
Oil for frying

Method

1 Slice and wash all vegetables.

2 Fry onions till tender.

3 Add all the other ingredients except the pasta.

4 Add water, bring to the boil and simmer till the vegetables are cooked.

5 Add the fine pasta and season.

This soup must be very thick and served hot with grated cheese.

Maltese Traditional Recipes

Timpana (Baked Macaroni in a Pastry Case)

Ingredients

1 lb macaroni
1 lb mixed ground beef and pork
1/2 lb chicken livers (optional)
1 lb flaky pastry or phyllo dough
2 large onions chopped
3 garlic cloves crushed
2 tbsp tomato paste
4 tbsp grated parmesan cheese
4 eggs lightly beaten
1/2 lb ricotta
Salt, pepper
Method
Prepare sauce: sauté onion and garlic in margarine. Add ground meat. Salt and pepper to taste. Stir well and cook for about 15 minutes.

Method

Add the tomato paste and a cup of beef stock. Simmer for an hour. Fry livers in margarine for 5 minutes.
Boil macaroni until barely tender. Rinse under cold water. Mix the Cooked meat and tomato mixture into the macaroni. Add ricotta, beaten eggs, and grated cheese. Season with salt and pepper to taste. Stir well.
Cover bottom and sides of a baking dish with pastry or phyllo dough.
Put in a layer of macaroni mixture. If you cooked chicken livers, arrange these over the macaroni and cover with another layer of macaroni.
Cover with pastry. Bake in 375 oven for an hour or until the top is brown. Let stand for half an hour before cutting in squares.

Maltese Traditional Recipes

Tomato Sauce with Meat and Eggs

Ingredients

200g onions

200g grated cheese

800g tomatoes

200g bacon

300g minced meat (pork or beef)

75g margarine

3 eggs

Salt and pepper

Method

1 Cut bacon in small pieces. Prepare the tomatoes by first peeling and then chopping them.

2 Slice and fry the onions, meat and bacon and continue cooking. Add tomatoes, salt and pepper. Cook for about 20 minutes.

3 before serving add the margarine, eggs and cheese.

4 Cook for 5 minutes. Serve warm.

Maltese Traditional Recipes

Vegetable Soup with Meat

Ingredients

100g cauliflower
50g celery stick
200g pork belly
50g white onions
20g tomato paste
50g rice
100g carrots
100g potatoes
2 lit water
100g cabbage
75g pumpkin
50g bacon
Salt and pepper
Oil for frying

Note: Pork can be replaced with Beef

Method

1 Slice and wash all the vegetables in very small pieces and place in different bowls.

2 Cook the onions in a medium sized pan. Do not brown. Add the remaining vegetables. Pour in the water and tomato paste.

3 Bring to the boil and then add meat. Simmer for 1½ hours.
4 Add the rice, salt and pepper 20 minutes before serving.

Maltese Traditional Recipes

Village Biscuits

Ingredients

200g flour

50g margarine

150g sugar

Pinch of cloves

1 egg

Royal icing

Grated orange and lemon zest

Pinch of cinnamon
Milk

Method
1 Mix the sieved flour and margarine until the mixture is like fine breadcrumbs.

2 Mix the egg, sugar and part of the milk. Add the zest, cloves and cinnamon to the flour. Add egg and make a smooth paste.

3 Grease a baking dish and sprinkle with the flour. Make oval shaped biscuits approximately 10cm x 6cm and about 1½cm thick.

4 Sprinkle some castor sugar on the biscuits and bake in moderate over for 20 minutes.
5 Cover to cook.
6 Decorate with piping of coloured royal icing.

Maltese Traditional Recipes

White Bait Poupiettes (Fish Patties)

Salmon or Tuna can be used, instead.

Ingredients

1/2 kg whitebait

A little crushed coriander

Garlic

One egg yolk

Chopped parsley

Oil

Seasoning

Flour or semolina

Method

Roughly cut the fish. Add the crushed garlic, coriander, parsley and egg. Mix well.

Add some flour to bind the mixture.

Divide into small balls.

Heat the oil, roll these balls in flour or semolina and fry on both sides till golden brown or until they are done.

Serve with tomato or tartar sauce.

Maltese Traditional Recipes

Widow's Soup

Ingredients

100g onions

50g tomato paste

150g peeled tomatoes

200g ricotta

100g potatoes

4 eggs
125g peas

125g cauliflower
Oil for frying

Method

1 Wash and slice all the vegetables.

2 Fry the onions, leaving them white.

3 Add the sliced cauliflower, tomato paste and chopped tomatoes.

2 Place mixtures into a pan, add water, peas, potatoes and seasoning. Bring to boil. Simmer till vegetables are cooked.

3 Add poached eggs. Cut ricotta into four pieces and add to the soup.
Cook for 5 minutes. Serve hot.

Maltese Traditional Recipes

Your Notes:

Maltese Traditional Recipes

Your Notes:

Maltese Traditional Recipes

Your Notes:

Maltese Traditional Recipes

Your Notes:

Made in the USA
Middletown, DE
28 August 2019